Spider

Spider

Written by **Sherry Been**

Illustrated by **Brad Davies**

This edition published in 2009 by Odyssey Books, a division of the Ciletti Publishing Group, Inc.

Printed by Pacifica Communications
Kyungee-Do, South Korea

Library of Congress Cataloging-in-Publication data is on file with the publisher.

Send all inquiries to:
Odyssey Books
463 Main St. Suite 200
Longmont, Colorado 80501

ISBN 978-0-9768655-5-1

1 2 3 4 5 6 7 8 9 10 PAC 10 09 08

About the Series

Get Wild! For Little People

This series has been designed for children ages four and up who are taking their first look at the world of animals. The text-to-self comparisons and anatomically correct illustrations offer a clear and consistent learning path for beginning and early readers. Each book presents valuable information about habitat, behavior, anatomy, diet, and reproduction in a way that makes learning fun.

If you were a spider,
we would call you
Great Spinner.

You build your web
between branches

or in the corner of an
old wooden shed.

You create squares,
diamond shapes,
and even **circular**
webs with great care.

Spiders live just
about everywhere.

Your **habitat**, or home, can be in mountains, deserts, and woods; grasslands, marshes, and even lakes.

If you were
a spider, we
would call
you **Arachnid**.

You are *not* an
insect.

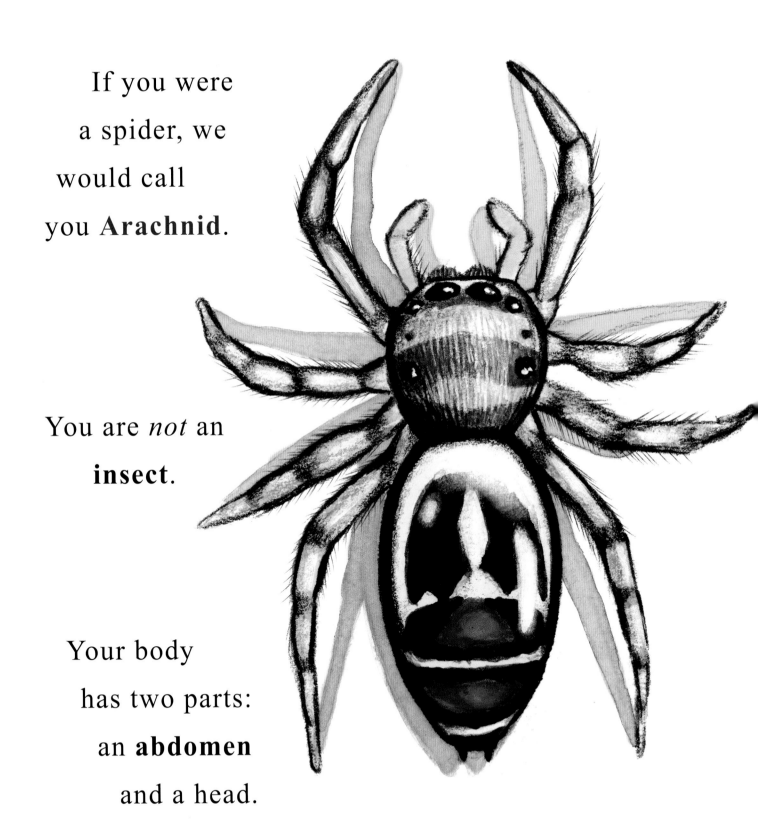

Your body
has two parts:
an **abdomen**
and a head.

Insect bodies have three parts:
a head, a chest, and an abdomen.

Arachnids do not have **antennae** or wings.
Insects have antennae and often have wings.

If you were a spider,
we would call you **Extreme!**

You could be almost too small to see,
or the size of a dinner plate.

With a leg span of
more than ten inches,
the Goliath bird-eating
spider eats
birds, mice,
and even
snakes.

When you are a spider,
you feel almost
everything
around you.

Your body and
eight legs are
covered
with
hairs so
sensitive

you can even feel the air!

As your **prey** gets near, you can sense it,
and then see it, long before it sees you.

If you were a spider, we would call you **Climber**.

Your feet have tufts of hair that let you walk on walls.

Most spiders have six or eight eyes.

Each one can look in its own direction.

This means that you can see several things at once.

Most other creatures can't do this.

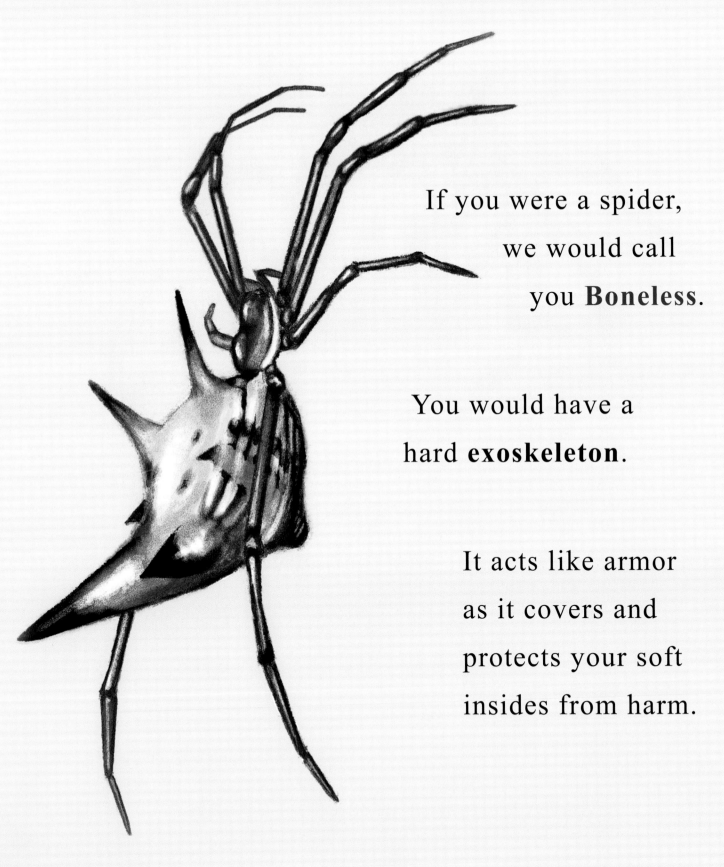

If you were a spider,
we would call
you **Boneless**.

You would have a
hard **exoskeleton**.

It acts like armor
as it covers and
protects your soft
insides from harm.

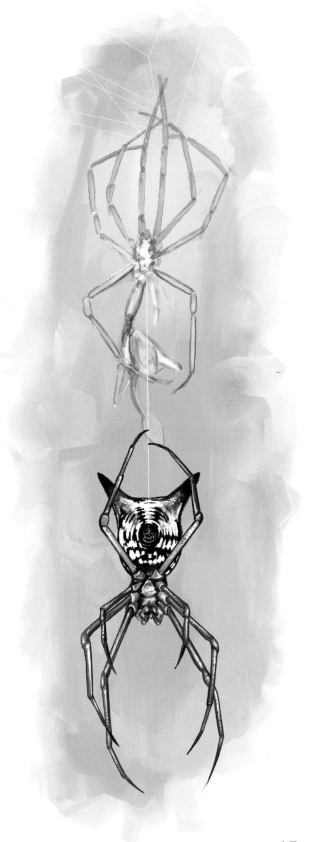

Your exoskeleton is also called a **carapace**. When you **molt,** it comes apart and a new one takes its place.

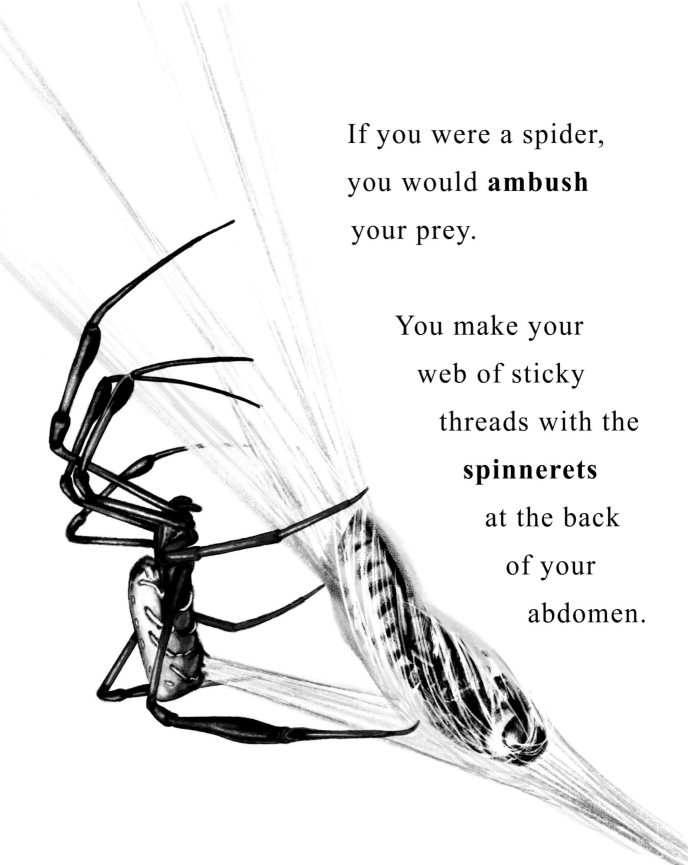

If you were a spider, you would **ambush** your prey.

You make your web of sticky threads with the **spinnerets** at the back of your abdomen.

18

You hide and wait. When your prey gets stuck in the sticky threads, you come running. You bite it. You wrap it up. You eat it right away or save it for later.

Through your
hollow fangs, you
inject poison into
your prey.

This paralyzes it so
it cannot fight or
get away.

Since you have no teeth
for chewing, you need to
drink your meal.

So your fangs then fill your catch with
liquid that turns its insides into jelly.

Pedipalps on both sides of your mouth hold your food while you suck that jelly into your belly.

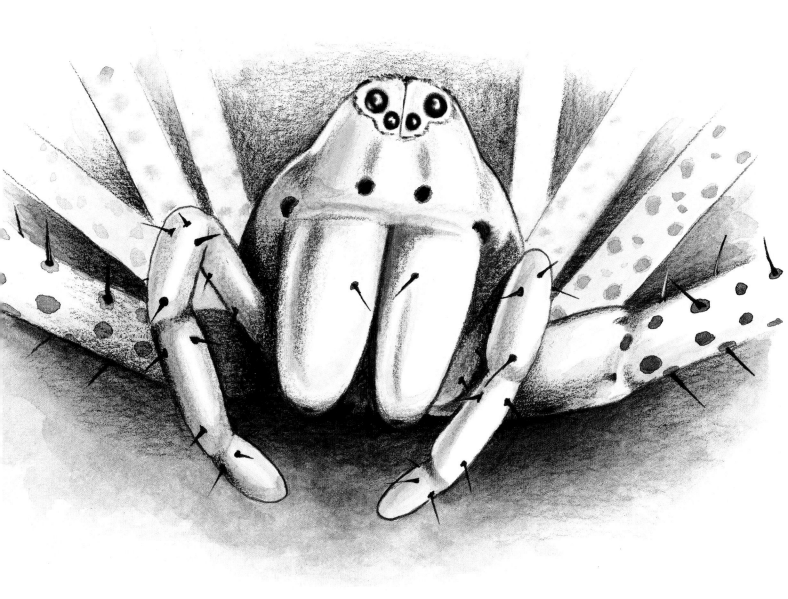

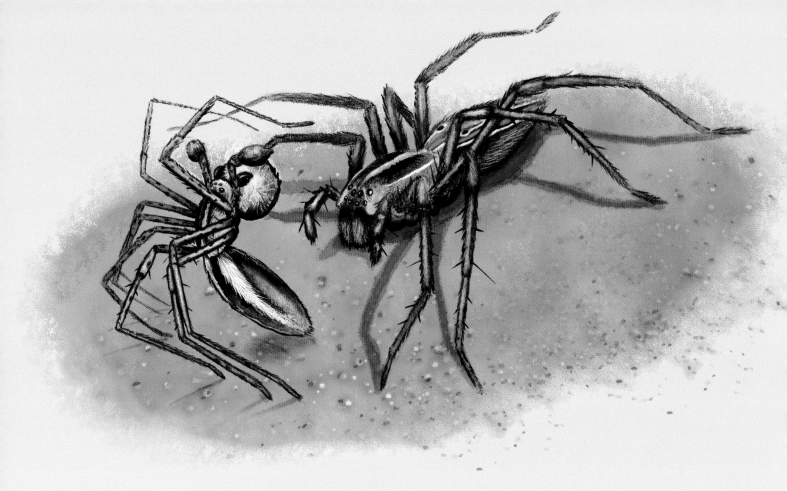

If you were a male spider,
you might dance for the female

or bring her food as a present
when you are ready to mate.

Once you fertilize her eggs, it's time to run.
Because she may try to eat you!

The female lays
hundreds of eggs.
She wraps them in
a silk sack that she
hides in a corner or
carries on her back
until they hatch.

If you were a
newly hatched
spider, we
would call you
Spiderling.

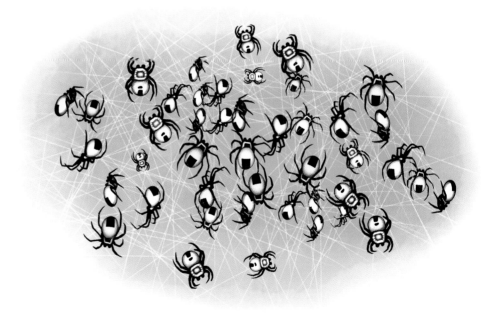

Spiderlings grow
quickly and
shed their
carapace
often to give
their growing
bodies more
space and
protection.

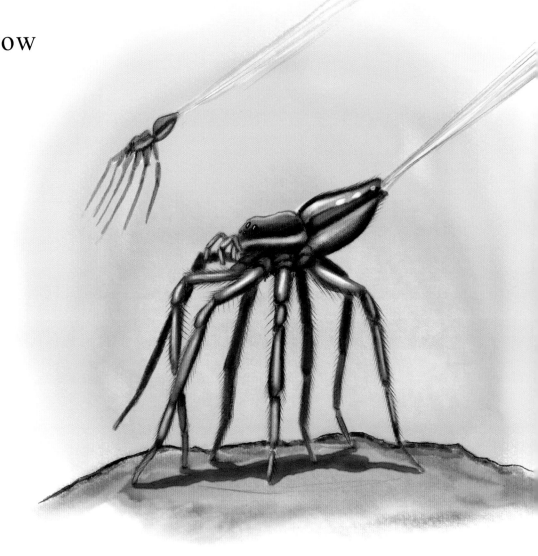

Rows of
eyes **develop**
along with the spinnerets used to make silk. Some
spiderlings can spin a silken thread that lets them leap
and float on the breeze. This is called ballooning.

The silk that spiders make is quite special. It is strong. It can be fat or thin, slippery or sticky; a perfect blanket for spider eggs, or even a trap. The net-casting spider throws a silken net on unsuspecting prey.

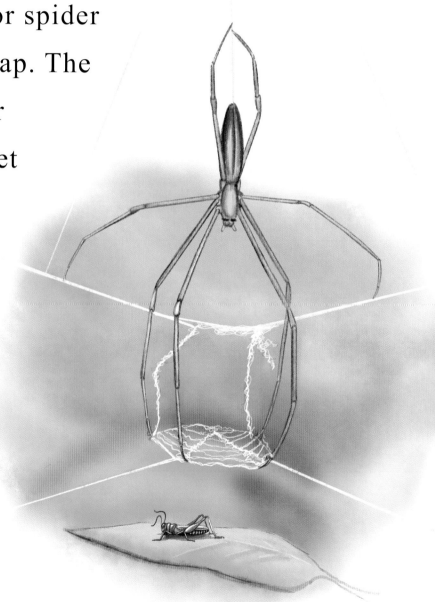

If you were
a spider, you
could make a
dragline that
lets you hang
from a leaf or
branch.

You seem to
disappear as you
prepare to attack
or hide from
danger.

Some of the creatures
you like to eat also
like to eat you!
Birds, lizards, and
even wasps eat
spiders.

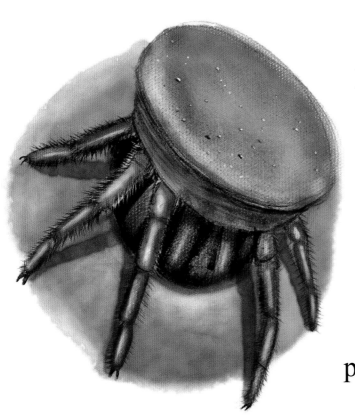

If you were a spider, you could be one of a great **variety**.

The trap-door spider hides in its burrow waiting to pounce on its prey.

The diving bell spider lives underwater in a silk bubble full of air.

The bola spider spits a sweet, sticky glob onto the end of a silk line to attract moths.

It swings the line around and around until a moth gets stuck.

Then it's time to eat!

If you were a black widow, we would call you **Deadly**! Your shiny black body with its red belly spot says **BEWARE!** Your poisonous bite can make even a large creature die.

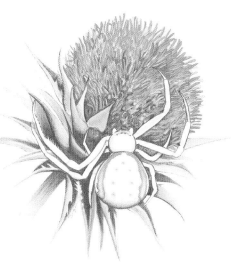

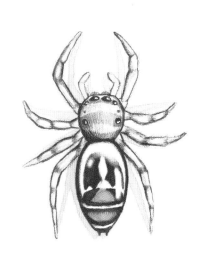

If you were a spider, we
would call you **Artist**.

You create.

You design
and **suspend**
amazing webs.
You are the
Great Spinner.

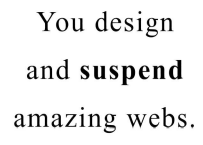

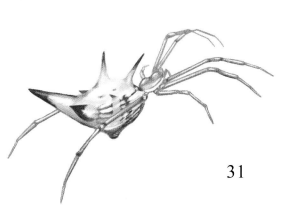

Spider Talk

abdomen	the entire rear portion of the body of insects and spiders
ambush	to hide, wait, and attack by surprise
antennae	a pair of movable sensory organs on the head of an insect
arachnid	an animal with no antennae and a segmented body divided into two main regions (for example, spider, scorpion, mite, and tick)
carapace	a hard case or shield covering all or part of an animal
circular	shaped like or nearly like a circle
develop	to go through a process of natural growth
dragline	a special kind of silk fiber that a spider can make
exoskeleton	a hard protective structure on the outside of a spider's body
habitat	the kind of place where an animal lives
inject	to force fluid into something
insect	an animal whose body is clearly divided into a head, thorax, and abdomen (for example, butterflies, grasshoppers, flies, and bees)
molt	to shed hair, feathers, outer skin, or shell so they can be replaced
pedipalps	leglike appendages near a spider's mouth used to hold food
prey	an animal that another creature hunts or catches
sensitive	touchy; easily stimulated
spinnerets	silk-spinning organs of a spider, silkworm, or insect larva
suspend	to hang
variety	having many different kinds